JEFFERSON

DAVIS

PRESIDENT OF THE CONFEDERACY

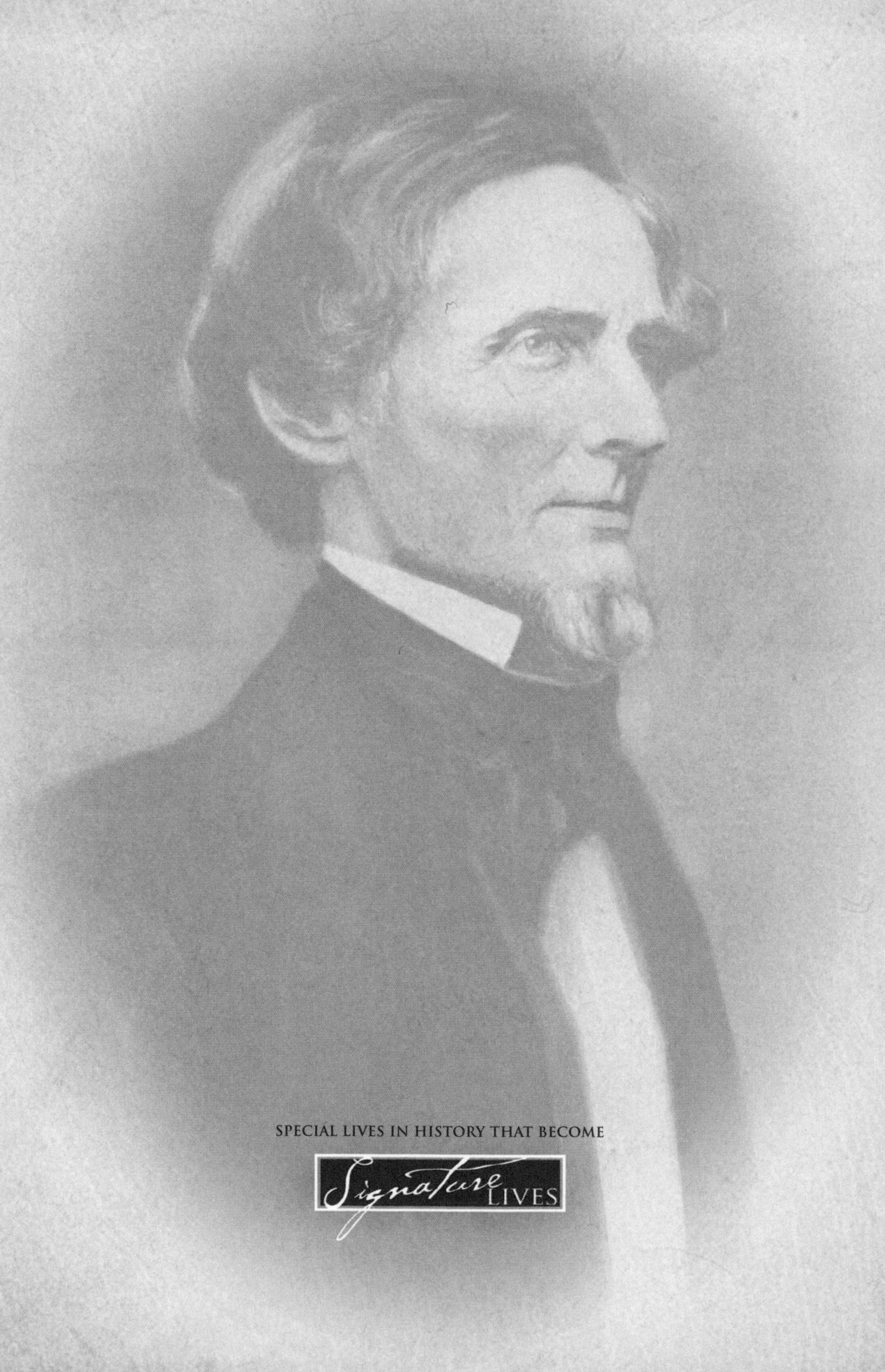

SPECIAL LIVES IN HISTORY THAT BECOME

Signature LIVES

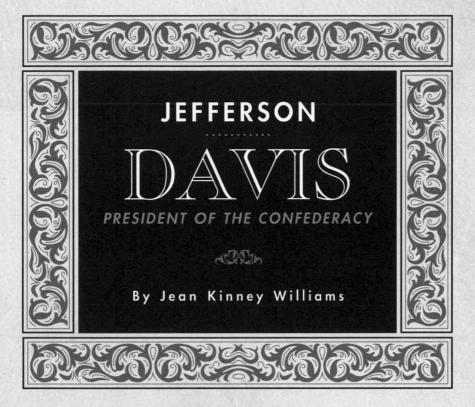

JEFFERSON
DAVIS
PRESIDENT OF THE CONFEDERACY

By Jean Kinney Williams

Content Adviser: Lisa Laskin, Ph.D.
Department of History
Harvard University

Reading Adviser: Rosemary G. Palmer, Ph.D.
Department of Literacy, College of Education
Boise State University

COMPASS POINT BOOKS ✦ MINNEAPOLIS, MINNESOTA

Compass Point Books
3109 West 50th Street, #115
Minneapolis, MN 55410

Visit Compass Point Books on the Internet at *www.compasspointbooks.com*
or e-mail your request to *custserv@compasspointbooks.com*

Editors: Heidi Schoof, Christianne Jones
Lead Designer: Jaime Martens
Photo researcher: Marcie C. Spence
Page production: Design Lab
Cartographer: XNR Productions, Inc.
Educational Consultant: Diane Smolinski

Managing Editor: Catherine Neitge
Art Director: Keith Griffin
Production Director: Keith McCormick
Creative Director: Terri Foley

JB
DAVIS, J.
C. 1

CIVIL WAR ERA

The Civil War (1861-1865) split the United States into two countries and divided the people over the issue of slavery. The opposing sides—the Union in the North and the Confederacy in the South—battled each other for four long years in the deadliest American conflict ever fought. The bloody war sometimes pitted family members and friends against each other over the issues of slavery and states' rights. Some of the people who lived and served their country during the Civil War are among the nation's most beloved heroes.

Jefferson Davis

Table of Contents

1 BREAKING AWAY

❧❧❧

On a cold January day in 1861, a United States senator faced his Washington colleagues for the last time. The visitors' section was packed that day to hear the emotional farewell speech of Senator Jefferson Davis of Mississippi.

> *"I rise for the purpose of announcing to the Senate that … the State of Mississippi, by a solemn ordinance of her people in convention assembled, has declared her separation from the United States. Under these circumstances, of course, my functions are terminated here."*

The people of Mississippi and other Southern states felt they had no choice but to secede, or leave the United States. With the election of antislavery Republican Abraham Lincoln as president, Southerners feared the federal government would override states' rights. This would mean the end of slavery. Plantation owners would have to set their slaves free or pay them for their work. Slavery was the South's way of life, and it had to be defended.

Jefferson Davis was known for his service to his country. As a young man, he distinguished himself in the Army, especially in the Mexican War. He served as secretary of war under President Franklin Pierce and was a prominent member of the U.S. Senate in the 1840s and 1850s. Davis considered himself a patriot who loved the United States. Still, on January 21, 1861, he gave up his U.S. citizenship and left Washington for Mississippi, which soon would be part of a new country: the Confederate States of America.

Near the end of his speech, Davis addressed the senators from the North, saying:

> *"I am sure there is not one of you, whatever sharp discussion there may have been between us, to whom I cannot now say, in the presence of my God, I wish you well; and such, I am sure, is the feeling of the people whom I represent towards those whom you represent. I therefore feel that I but express their desire when I say I hope, and*

they hope, for peaceful relations with you, though we must part. ... The reverse may bring disaster on every portion of the country."

The disaster that resulted came in the form of America's deadliest conflict—the Civil War. Because of his leadership abilities and his firm belief in states' rights and slavery, Jefferson Davis was chosen to serve as president of the Confederacy during the Civil War. It is these four years for which he is remembered, despite many earlier accomplishments.

2 GROWING SOUTHERN ROOTS

❧❀❧

Born June 3, 1808, in Christian County, Kentucky, Jefferson Davis was the 10th and last child of Revolutionary War patriot Samuel E. Davis. Samuel and his wife, Jane Cook Davis, moved their family west from Georgia to Kentucky after the Revolutionary War. There they cleared land for a farm and built the log cabin where their youngest son was born. Jefferson F. Davis was named for his father's political hero, Thomas Jefferson. No one knows for sure what the "F" stood for.

Around 1810, Samuel moved his family briefly to Louisiana and then to Mississippi. There he became a cotton farmer with the help of his children and the dozen or so slaves that he owned. Though Samuel Davis never became wealthy, he built a comfortable

Large pillars and wraparound porches adorned many Mississippi plantation homes in the 1800s.

home on the farm he called Poplar Grove and was able to send Jefferson away to boarding school.

St. Thomas College, Jefferson's new school in Kentucky, was a Catholic elementary school. Davis was a bright student and enjoyed his two years at St. Thomas. He studied Latin, ancient Greek, history, and science. Jefferson's parents missed him, so he returned home at the age of 10 to attended the nearby Wilkinson County Academy.

One day, young Jefferson decided he'd had enough of school and announced he was going to quit. Samuel Davis wanted to teach his son a lesson about the value of education, so he didn't argue with him. Instead, he sent him out to the fields to spend a day picking cotton with the slaves. By the end of that day, school seemed much more appealing to Jefferson, and he changed his mind about quitting.

In the spring of 1823, 14-year-old Jefferson Davis returned to Kentucky to attend Transylvania University in Lexington. Located in the rolling hills of central Kentucky, the university offered studies in history, literature, languages, and sciences, as well as medicine and law. Jefferson's parents paid about $200 for their son to live at the university and attend school there.

Jefferson enjoyed his days at Transylvania, but they ended abruptly when his father died in the summer of 1824. Heartbroken at losing his father, Jefferson returned to Mississippi. During

Transylvania University was established in 1780.

his time at home, Jefferson was appointed by President James Monroe to attend West Point military academy. Instead of returning to Transylvania, 16-year-old Jefferson reported as a

Firing exercises were part of the cadets training at West Point.

cadet to the U.S. Military Academy at West Point, New York, in September.

Life at West Point was a challenge for its all-male student body. Jefferson struggled with mathematics, a very important subject at the military academy. The school's strict rules allowed students just one visit home during their four-year stay. The school expected its students to live by its motto, "Duty, Honor, Country."

Many students dropped out of West Point, but those who stayed, like Davis, formed strong bonds with each other. Two classmates in particular, Robert E. Lee and Albert Sidney Johnston, would play important roles in Davis's later life.

In 1802, President Thomas Jefferson signed papers to establish the U.S. Military Academy at West Point. It is the oldest continuously occupied military post in the United States.

Though Davis graduated from West Point with average grades, he was a popular student and had acquired a code of self-discipline that would last him a lifetime.

After graduating in June 1828, he returned to Mississippi for a rare visit with his family. On December 31, 1828, Second Lieutenant Davis reported for duty at Jefferson Barracks, an Army training post just south of St. Louis, Missouri.

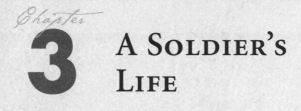

3 A SOLDIER'S LIFE

❧❦❧

After training at Jefferson Barracks, Davis was assigned to a series of frontier forts in what was then the country's Northwest. He was among the first white Americans to visit the wilderness area of northern Illinois and Wisconsin. He showed leadership ability as he helped to settle problems between white settlers and Native Americans.

Problems between Native Americans and white settlers hightened when the government ordered the Native Americans to leave their land in northern Illionois and go to Iowa. In April 1832, famous Sauk chief, Black Hawk, led his Sauk tribe against the government's orders.

Black Hawk's people were starving, and food was running out in Iowa. Black Hawk led his people from Iowa back to Illinois to plant corn. Soldiers stopped the returning tribe and started attacking them. At that moment, the Black Hawk War began.

The final battle of the Black Hawk War took place at the Bad Axe River in Wisconsin. Black Hawk and his tribe were cornered, and 950 Sauk were killed.

Black Hawk escaped at first, but was soon captured and handed over to Colonel Zachary Taylor at Fort Crawford in Prairie du Chien, Wisconsin. Black Hawk and his followers had attempted to reclaim their homeland in Illinois, refusing the U.S. government's order to move west to Iowa. Jefferson Davis sympathized with Black Hawk and his people but was assigned to escort the prisoners south to Jefferson Barracks in St. Louis. Along the way, Davis and Black Hawk became friends. The chief later praised Davis as "a good and brave young chief" who tried to protect Black Hawk from curious white visitors eager to see him.

While stationed at Fort Crawford, Jefferson met and fell in love with Sarah Knox Taylor. She was the charming daughter of his commanding officer (and

> *During the Black Hawk War, about 3,000 U.S. soldiers pursued Black Hawk and his Sauk tribe. The tribe consisted of about 500 men and 500 women and children. Although Black Hawk and his tribe were greatly outnumbered, the Black Hawk War lasted 118 days.*

future president) Zachary Taylor. Sarah, often called Knox or Knoxie, was born at Fort Knox in Vincennes, Indiana, in 1814. She was named Sarah after her grandmother and Knox after the fort where she was born. Colonel Taylor was against the relationship between Jefferson and

Fort Crawford in Prairie du Chien, Wisconsin, was established by the U.S. Army in 1816.

Sarah, partly because of a disagreement between him and Davis, but more importantly, he wanted his daughter to escape the hardships of military life. But Knox was an educated young woman who wasn't afraid to stand up to her father, and the relationship continued.

In 1834, Davis was sent to Fort Gibson in present-day Oklahoma. There he joined the newly formed First Dragoons—an Army unit assigned to protect white settlers from Native Americans as the frontier moved west. Although his promotion to first lieutenant meant a pay raise for Jefferson, leaving Wisconsin also meant leaving Sarah behind.

The Dragoons spent that first cold winter sleeping in tents. The next summer they traveled the countryside where temperatures reached more than 100 F (38 C). During this time, Jefferson and Sarah kept in touch through letters.

In 1835, Davis resigned from the Army, perhaps because Sarah's parents didn't want their daughter to marry a soldier. Davis had a new plan.

He was going to become a cotton farmer like his oldest brother, Joseph. Despite rumors that they had eloped, Jefferson Davis and Sarah Knox Taylor were married in a private, formal ceremony on June 17, 1835. The wedding took place at Beechland, the home of Sarah's Aunt Elizabeth, near Louisville, Kentucky. The newlyweds traveled to Vicksburg, Mississippi, by steamboat to visit Joseph and begin planning their life together.

Malaria is spread by the bite of a mosquito that carries the infection. Symptoms are flu-like and include fever, chills, headache, muscle aches, tiredness, nausea, vomiting, and diarrhea. Infection with one deadly type of malaria, if not promptly treated, may cause kidney failure, seizures, mental confusion, coma, and death.

Later that summer, they paid a visit to Jefferson's oldest sister, Anna Smith, at Locust Grove, her home in West Feliciana Parish, Louisiana. During this trip, both Jefferson and Sarah came down with a deadly form of malaria. Sarah Knox Taylor Davis, just 21 years old, died on September 15, two days before the couple's three-month anniversary. Jefferson remained ill for many weeks after Sarah's death. ✍

4 STARTING OVER

ം⌇⌇ം

As he tried to recover from his illness and the loss of his young bride, Davis spent the winter of 1835-36 relaxing in Havana, Cuba. The balmy weather was much better for his health. He then returned to Mississippi, where he lived quietly for the next several years, building up his cotton plantation along the Mississippi River.

Davis received 900 acres (360 hectares) of untouched land from his brother Joseph. Joseph was a successful lawyer in Natchez, Mississippi, who eventually became one of the state's wealthiest men. Joseph owned thousands of acres on "Davis Bend," a strip of rich farmland nearly surrounded by the Mississippi River. Joseph also owned as many as 350 slaves, who worked on

Slaves worked and lived on Jefferson Davis's plantation in Mississippi.

the plantation he called Hurricane. Until now, Jefferson Davis had owned only one slave—a man named James Pemberton. He had accompanied Davis on his Army assignments and was a trusted servant. He became the overseer, or slave supervisor, on the plantation Davis named Brierfield. With approximately $10,000 borrowed from Joseph, Jefferson went to Natchez where he bought 16 black men and women. By 1840, Jefferson Davis owned 40 slaves.

Slaves worked all day picking cotton. They had few breaks from the hot sun.

Like most Southern plantation owners, the Davis brothers saw nothing wrong with keeping slaves. It was legal, and many believed it was the best way of life in the United States. But Jefferson and his brother Joseph treated their slaves better than many plantation owners. The Davis slaves were given positions of authority and responsibility on the plantations, and Jefferson Davis would not allow whips used on his slaves. He kept his slave families together and gave each a garden in which to grow produce to sell. Davis knew that many slave owners weren't as good to their slaves, yet no amount of abolitionist argument before or after the Civil War could change his mind about slavery.

Because of their loyalty to Thomas Jefferson, founder of the Democratic Party, Joseph and Jefferson Davis were almost the only Democrats in a region that strongly supported the Whig Party. Democrats insisted that the national government should not interfere with the rights of individual states— including the right to keep slaves. The Whig Party, on the other hand, favored a stronger national government with more control over the states.

In his free time, Jefferson spent hours in his brother's library, reading books on economics and political philosophy by famous writers such as John Locke and Thomas Jefferson. He read plays by William Shakespeare and poetry by Lord Byron and Robert Burns. He also enjoyed his brother's company as they discussed the running of their plantations or, a subject of growing interest to Jefferson, American politics.

With his new interest in politics, Jefferson Davis began attending state Democratic meetings. In 1843, with the election just days away, he agreed to run for the state's House of Representatives against a strong Whig candidate, Seargent S. Prentiss. Though he lost, the 35-year-old Davis impressed party leaders and even his Whig opponents with his spirited campaign and effective speaking. One local newspaper, which supported Democrats, predicted Davis had a proud and honorable career in politics ahead of him.

Davis continued his involvement with Democratic politics. In January 1844, he enthused the crowd at a statewide Democratic convention with a speech supporting Senator John C. Calhoun for U.S. president. The senator from South Carolina was a fiery speaker whom many considered the unofficial spokesman for the South (a title later inherited by Jefferson Davis). According to Davis, Calhoun was the ideal candidate: he believed in strengthening the power of the states and favored a low tariff—a tax on goods that were imported or exported. Southerners felt that such taxes favored the industrial Northern states and caused European countries to buy less cotton from the American

South. Senator Calhoun also wanted to expand the country by making Texas a state.

The annexation of Texas was a sensitive issue. Since Texas would enter the United States as a slave state, many Northerners opposed it. Jefferson Davis was in favor of annexing Texas. He knew it would increase the number of pro-slavery representatives in Congress.

With his political career off to a promising start, Jefferson made a fresh start in his personal life as well. Varina Banks Howell, the daughter of a good friend of Joseph's, arrived at Hurricane in 1844 for a visit to her Uncle Joe. Joseph had worried about Jefferson, who was still mourning for Sarah after eight years. Some historians believe he may have been playing matchmaker by inviting Varina for an extended stay. Joseph felt that Jefferson had a real future in politics, and he knew that Jefferson would be looked upon more favorably if he were married. Varina Howell was from a

Varina Banks Howell Davis, 1849

powerful family and was well educated in politics, literature, languages, and philosophy. She was also very beautiful.

Though Varina was barely 18 when she met Jefferson Davis, who was almost 36, he impressed her greatly. Varina wrote her mother soon after their meeting:

"I do not know whether this Mr. Jefferson Davis is young or old. He looks both at times; but I believe he is old, for from what I hear he is only two years younger than you are [the rumor was correct]. He impresses me as a remarkable kind of man, but of uncertain temper, and has a way of taking for granted that everybody agrees with him when he expresses an opinion."

Davis was lighthearted and friendly, and Varina's heart raced when she watched him. Davis was equally taken with the intelligent young woman, and within a month they were engaged.

Varina and her parents felt that Davis was perfect in every way but one: he was a Democrat. The Howells were Whigs, and they raised their daughter to believe this was the "correct" party for people of their social standing. Also, women of that time were considered an extension of their husbands and were expected to support their political ideas. However, when Jefferson asked Varina's parents for her hand in marriage, they decided that the kind of man he was mattered much more than his political party. Davis and Varina were married at the Howells home in Natchez on February 26, 1845. Varina had learned a great deal about the Democratic party and was ready to stand by her husband's political principles.

Jefferson Davis and Varina Howell Davis posed for a portrait after their wedding in 1845.

That fall, Jefferson Davis was elected to the U.S. House of Representatives by the state of Mississippi. But Davis's stay in Washington was interrupted by war. Many Democrats believed that it was America's "Manifest Destiny" to control all the land between Mexico, Canada, and the Atlantic and Pacific oceans. Many Whigs, on the other hand, considered this idea too aggressive. President James K. Polk put Manifest Destiny to the test in May 1846 by declaring war on Mexico over the desirable land of California.

Davis supported the war and returned to the Army with the rank of colonel. He left Washington to take command of a Mississippi regiment. He took with him a black servant named Jim Green and an Arabian horse, both provided by Joseph. He had given James Pemberton the choice of going to Mexico or staying behind to run Brierfield. Pemberton chose to stay in Mississippi.

The U.S. military, under Zachary Taylor, captured Monterrey during the Mexican War in 1846.

Davis rejoined his former commander and father-in-law Zachary Taylor, now a major general, at Brazos Island, at the southern tip of Texas. The two men developed a warm friendship, and Taylor took

a keen interest in Davis's regiment, nicknamed the Mississippi Rifles for the special guns Davis provided them with. After a few weeks of drills and training, General Taylor and his troops moved into Mexico.

Davis and the Mississippi Rifles played key roles in two important American victories during the Mexican War. On September 21, 1846, the Mississippians, along with a Tennessee regiment, stormed a fort at Monterrey, Mexico. As gunfire rained upon them, they took the fort and continued to fight their way through the streets of Monterrey.

On February 22, 1847, at Buena Vista, Mexico, Taylor's army faced the much larger army of Mexico's highest ranking general, Antonio Lopez de Santa Anna. A bold charge by the Mississippi riflemen and Indiana volunteers under Colonel Davis sealed the American victory. Davis, who fought alongside his men as he cheered them on, was shot in the ankle at Buena Vista. But the pain of his battle wound was outweighed by the pride he felt in his regiment and, more important, the hero's welcome he received upon returning home. ✺

5 STORMS IN THE SENATE

❦

In August 1847, Jefferson Davis became a U.S. senator for Mississippi. Governor Albert G. Brown appointed Davis after the death of a senator, which left a Senate seat vacant. Davis took the Senate oath on crutches because of his battle wound.

Though satisfying, Davis's return to Washington, D.C., wasn't easy. Varina remained at home in Mississippi. Davis's ankle injury continued to be painful, and he was often feverish since his 1835 case of malaria. But unlike many first-year senators and representatives, Davis spoke up freely in Senate discussions, especially on the subject of slavery.

Davis and others believed that the right to own slaves was included in the constitutional rights concerning property—with slaves being

Fights between congressmen who disagreed were common in the mid-1800s.

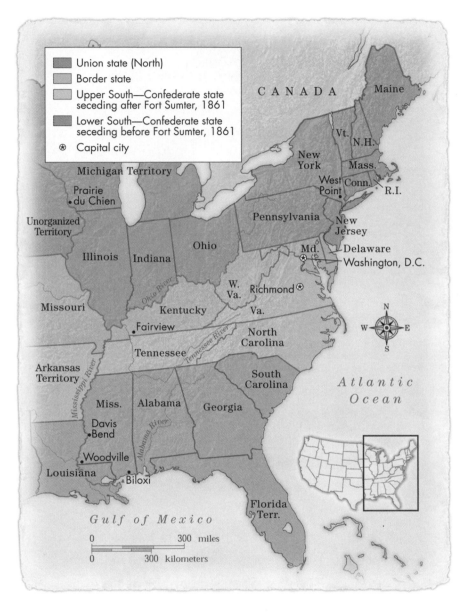

Davis owned a lot of land in Mississippi, which was one of the slave states.

considered property. Those opposing slavery generally claimed the Constitution didn't formally mention it because its writers disapproved of it.

As the nation acquired new territories and spread westward, slavery dominated all other issues in national politics. The arguments centered on the admission of new states to the Union as either free or slave states, and the resulting balance of power between North and South. The Missouri Compromise of 1820 had quieted this debate for many years, at least in regard to the territory acquired by the U.S. in the Louisiana Purchase.

When the Missouri Territory was being considered for statehood in 1819, there was an equal number of free states and slave states in the Union. The Mason-Dixon Line determined the border between Maryland and Pennsylvania. This line was simply a survey line, but many people saw it as a line that separated the free states from the slave states.

The Missouri Compromise defined the future boundary between slave and free states in the Louisiana Purchase territory. Congress admitted Missouri as a slave state on the condition that no other slave states could be

The Louisiana Purchase of 1803 is called the greatest real estate deal in history. The United States paid France $15 million for the Louisiana Territory, which nearly doubled the size of the United States. This 828,000-square-mile (2,152,800-square-kilometer) territory stretched from the Mississippi River to the Rocky Mountains and from the Gulf of Mexico to the Canadian border. Thirteen new states were eventually formed from this territory.

formed from territory north of the 36 degrees 30 minutes north latitude line, Missouri's southern border. At the same time, Maine was admitted as a new free state, preserving the balance between slave and free.

After the Mexican War, with the addition of new land to the west of the Louisiana Purchase, the issue of slavery expansion again demanded attention. Southerners in Congress, including Davis, signed a declaration of unity against abolitionist attacks and called for an equal number of free and slave states in the new territories. They were furious when President Zachary Taylor, a fellow slave owner from Louisiana, supported the admission of California as a free state. After all, Davis argued, Southerners had fought hard—and died—in the Mexican War to acquire California. All should be able to enjoy the territory, with or without slaves.

By 1849, immigration had swelled the population of many Northern states. These states now could send more representatives to Congress. Each state, however, was only allowed to send two senators regardless of population, and the Senate remained evenly split between 15 free and 15 slave states. Southern senators were fearful of becoming completely overpowered by antislavery senators if more slave states weren't added.

In 1850, with California statehood at the center of growing North and South disagreements, Kentucky Senator Henry Clay (author of the Missouri Compromise of 1820) was determined to find a solution. On January 29, Clay presented another compromise. Led by elder statesmen Clay,

Daniel Webster from Massachusetts, and South Carolina's John C. Calhoun, members of Congress spent eight months debating the slavery issue. Senator Stephen Douglas, a young Democrat from Illinois, assisted in preparing the series of bills that would make up the compromise.

California would be admitted as a free state, but the people of the New Mexico, Arizona, Nevada, and Utah territories would vote on slavery when admitted as states. Northern lawmakers strongly supported outlawing slavery in Washington, D.C., because it seemed dishonest to allow slavery in the capital of a country dedicated to personal freedom. According to the compromise, slavery would still be permitted in Washington, but the selling of slaves would not. In order to please the slave-state politicians, a very controversial bill was included in the Compromise of 1850: the Fugitive Slave Act. This act required all citizens to help in the recovery of escaped slaves.

The compromise struggle lasted until the Senate adjourned in September. Davis strongly disapproved of the compromise solutions during the debates. He wanted the Missouri Compromise line extended straight west, and he protested California's admission as a free state. Congress, he claimed, was taking away his constitutional right as a slave owner to move about the country with his "property."

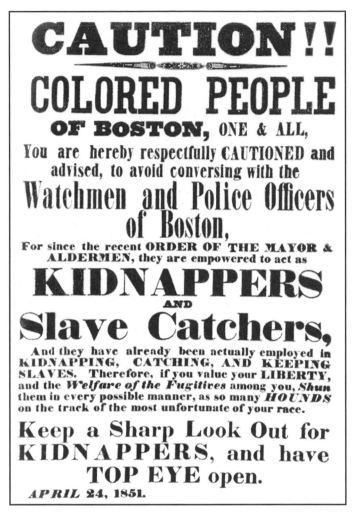

CAUTION!!
COLORED PEOPLE
OF BOSTON, ONE & ALL,

You are hereby respectfully CAUTIONED and advised, to avoid conversing with the

Watchmen and Police Officers of Boston,

For since the recent ORDER OF THE MAYOR & ALDERMEN, they are empowered to act as

KIDNAPPERS
AND
Slave Catchers,

And they have already been actually employed in KIDNAPPING, CATCHING, AND KEEPING SLAVES. Therefore, if you value your LIBERTY, and the *Welfare of the Fugitives* among you, *Shun* them in every possible manner, as so many *HOUNDS* on the track of the most unfortunate of your race.

Keep a Sharp Look Out for KIDNAPPERS, and have TOP EYE open.

APRIL 24, 1851.

A flyer printed in 1851 was passed throughout Boston warning African-Americans of the newly enforced Fugitive Slave Act.

Although Davis voted for the Fugitive Slave Act, he returned home to Mississippi dismayed with the Compromise of 1850.

In fall of 1851, Southern-rights supporters approached Davis to run for governor of Mississippi. Davis, at home while the Senate was in recess, was

Jefferson and Varina enjoyed spending time together at their Brierfield plantation.

again struggling with a fever. He also suffered from a painful eye condition, often during times of stress, which could keep him in a darkened room for weeks at a time. Nevertheless, Davis quit his Senate seat to accept the nomination for governor. Though his health kept him home at first, Jefferson dictated letters to Varina for publication and later managed campaign speeches as voting day approached. He softened his stand against the Compromise of 1850, yet encouraged Mississippians to fight the passing of antislavery laws. His opponent, Henry Foote, won the election in a close race. Though Davis emerged from the race with plenty of popularity, he stepped back from politics and returned to his Brierfield plantation.

Davis and Varina had built a comfortable home with nine rooms and wide porches. The couple now enjoyed some rare leisure time together—riding horses in the countryside, visiting with neighbors, or reading.

In July 1852, after seven years of marriage, Jefferson and Varina were thrilled to welcome their first child, a son. They named him Samuel Emory after Jefferson's father.

Davis kept his hand in politics by campaigning for the Democratic nominee for president, Franklin Pierce. Davis and Pierce had been friends in Congress, and both served under Zachary Taylor in the Mexican War. Pierce defeated Whig candidate Winfield Scott in the November election. He offered Davis the Cabinet position of secretary of war, which Davis accepted early in 1853.

> *The race for president in the election of 1852 wasn't much of a race. The Whig party was losing steam, which gave the Democrats a huge advantage. Neither candidate took a stand on issues, leaving little for people to vote on. Instead, both candidates focused on mudslinging, or spreading rumors about the other candidate. Franklin Pierce ended up winning by a landslide.*

6 SECRETARY OF WAR

❦❧

Jefferson Davis is considered one of the country's most capable war secretaries (a position known today as the secretary of defense). Though many of his policies benefited the South, Davis also showed that he viewed the United States as a whole. For example, he strengthened and increased the size of the existing Army. He introduced new military tactics for training and modernized the weapons supply, adding a new and more deadly type of bullet, the "minié ball." Army pay was increased, and a medical corps was established. Davis also worked with former West Point classmate Robert E. Lee, now the school's director, to improve training there. He even experimented with camels in the Southwest for desert transport.

As secretary of war, Jefferson Davis also took time for minor details: when West Point seniors requested permission to grow beards, Davis answered them personally. The answer was no, in part because past military leaders such as George Washington and Andrew Jackson had been clean-shaven.

Cadets at West Point take a break from training to pose for a picture.

Jefferson Davis was an influential member of the Pierce administration and performed his duties with characteristic energy and ability, though he occasionally butted heads with the Army's commanding general, Winfield Scott. Davis worked to improve railroads in the South and river navigation on the lower Mississippi. He arranged to buy a strip of land in the Southwest from Mexico in order to put a railroad through it.

Both Jefferson and Varina enjoyed the stimulation of Washington life. Varina's warmth as a friend, contrasted with her sometimes sarcastic and biting wit, won her friends and foes alike. The family was shattered, though, in June 1854 when little Sam died from measles. Jefferson and Varina, who had waited so long for children, were heartbroken. But by February 1855, another child, a daughter, was born. Margaret "Maggie" Howell Davis was named after Varina's mother. Maggie was followed two years later by a brother, Jefferson Jr.

About the same time that the Davis family returned to Washington, Harriet Beecher Stowe published a novel that blazed across the nation: Uncle Tom's Cabin. Stowe had lived in Cincinnati, a main station on the Underground Railroad, and she wrote a story about the cruel institution of slavery that existed just across the Ohio River in Kentucky. The book was a sensation and fueled growing antislavery sentiments in the North.

"Tragic Prelude" by John Steuart Curry shows John Brown leading anti-slavery forces to keep Kansas a free state.

The slave-versus-free state issue heated up once again with the passing of the Kansas-Nebraska Act of 1854. Congress declared that the residents of Kansas and Nebraska, which were set to become states, could decide whether to allow slavery, much like New Mexico and Utah before them. Nebraska quietly rejected slavery, while events in Kansas foreshadowed what the nation would endure with the Civil War. Pro-slavery Missourians came to Kansas to vote for pro-slavery laws, while abolitionists moved to

Kansas from the east to vote against slavery. Lawless violence marked Kansas's early years.

Franklin Pierce was not renominated for president, in part because of his weak handling of the Kansas situation. Democrats instead nominated James Buchanan. His opponent, John C. Frémont, was a member of a new party called the Republicans. The Republican Party was formed in the North to fight the spread of slavery, but it also included Whig beliefs such as higher tariffs. Though Frémont lost the 1856 presidential election, Southerners were alarmed at how many votes he received in the North—a sign of the deepening divide.

In March 1857, shortly before Buchanan's inauguration, Jefferson Davis handed Pierce his resignation as secretary of war. He then walked to the Capitol to be sworn into the Senate, having been elected to that position again by the Mississippi legislature. It would be his last U.S. government position. ॐ

7 THE MONSTER CRISIS BEGINS

❧❧❧

In Mississippi, Jefferson Davis told his constituents that a monster crisis for the United States could result from the next election. More and more Southerners were threatening to break away from the United States if a Republican won the presidency in 1860. One member of the new Republican Party, Abraham Lincoln, responded to Southern threats to secede saying, "We won't let you. With the purse and the sword, the army and navy and treasury in our hands and at our command, you couldn't do it."

In March 1857, a Supreme Court opinion, often called the Dred Scott decision, added fuel to the fire. Dred Scott was a Missouri slave whose owner took him to free territory before returning to Missouri.

Dred Scott was a brave and patient man. It took 10 years of appeals for him to get his case brought before the Supreme Court.

Scott, having lived north of the 36 degree 30 minute line, sued for his freedom. The Supreme Court heard his case and not only decided against his claim, but also declared Congress had no right to limit slavery in the territories, throwing out the Missouri Compromise and the 36 degree 30 minute line. The decision also stated that slaves were not citizens and had no rights as citizens.

Southerners like Davis rejoiced—the court, it seemed, had settled the thorny issue of whether slavery could spread beyond the present slave states. Davis always considered laws limiting slavery as unconstitutional. The Dred Scott decision allowed him to continue to imagine the expansion of American slavery well into the future.

By this time, Davis was one of the Senate's most prominent members. He was also among the most educated. *New York Tribune* newspaper editor Horace Greeley called Jefferson Davis "unquestionably the foremost man of the South today," as well as the "most formidable" foe in the debate against slavery.

In February 1858, Davis was again suffering with his painful eye trouble and forced to spend two months in bed in a darkened room. He was visited often by New York senator and abolitionist leader, William Seward. Davis and Seward had been friends for many years, in spite of their differences.

The North-South conflict that boiled in Kansas spilled over into the Senate. In one incident, antislavery Senator Charles Sumner of Massachusetts insulted South Carolina Senator Andrew Butler in a speech called "The Crime against Kansas." A few days later, Sumner was attacked and severely beaten by Butler's young cousin, South Carolina Representative Preston S. Brooks. Sumner spent three years recovering from his injuries before returning to his seat in the Senate.

Jefferson Davis was an honest man who spoke with great conviction.

They differed, of course, on slavery. They also differed in the way they carried out their political business. Seward excelled at the making of deals and behind-the-scenes politics. This was something Jefferson Davis never mastered—even his critics admired his honesty about his beliefs. "But, Mr. Seward, do you never speak from conviction?" Davis asked him once. "Never," Seward answered lightheartedly. Davis replied, "As God is my judge, I never speak from any other motive." Seward knew he meant it.

Davis was back at his Senate desk in May 1858. That summer, Jefferson, Varina, and the children left behind the sticky heat of Washington, D.C., to travel in the Northeast. Maine's cool breezes and fresh air sped Davis's recovery along. He took advantage of this opportunity to address Northern audiences in an attempt to bridge the North-South gap. Davis stressed his patriotism and reminded his audience how the states had helped one another in the Revolutionary War.

Slavery was an issue for each state to decide—he wouldn't tell the people of Maine how to live. In Boston, the center of the abolitionist movement, he defended slavery, saying, "For servitude is the only agency through which Christianity has reached that degraded race, the only means by which they have been civilized and elevated." He argued that neither the Bible nor the Constitution outlawed slavery. He came away from his tour thinking the number of pro-South sympathizers in the North was stronger than it really was, perhaps because he often addressed Democratic audiences.

In April 1859, a new baby, Joseph Evan Davis, joined the family. Though nearly 51, Jefferson took great delight in his small children. He and Varina enjoyed a warm, loving marriage.

As 1860 approached, Davis's concern over the Republican Party grew. He accused Lincoln of driving a bigger wedge between North and South. On the other hand, the "fire-eaters," the zealous Southerners demanding secession, were increasingly vocal. Davis still considered himself a moderate and pro-Union Southerner, yet he could heat up the public discussion as well as any fire-eater. Compromise, it seemed, was something for the other side to do.

By the late 1850s, almost any issue Congress addressed eventually touched back on North-South divisions. Stephen Douglas proposed popular sovereignty, in which states and territories would make their own decisions on slavery. Southern lawmakers now demanded a slave code, or laws protecting the rights of slave owners. It may have been the stress of the times that caused Jefferson's health to plague him. One reporter described him as a brave sufferer who always appeared to be in anguish.

In October 1859, a radical abolitionist named

> *Although abolitionist John Brown wasn't a wealthy man, he traveled to many states to speak against and fight slavery. At one point, Brown even had to file for bankruptcy. However, this did not stop Brown from supporting the issues he believed in, especially antislavery. He would raise the money needed to fight for rights and find people to fight with him.*

John Brown attempted to take on the South almost single-handedly. He and his band of about 20 men—including his own sons and five black men—captured the federal government's arsenal at

John Brown holds one of his dying sons at Harpers Ferry

Harpers Ferry, Virginia (today it's in West Virginia). Brown hoped to take arms from the arsenal and establish a base in the nearby Appalachian Mountains. From there he planned to recruit fugitive slaves to help attack Southern slaveholders. All he managed to do before being captured, however, was cause chaos in Harpers Ferry. Brown was captured by Confederate Colonel Robert E. Lee and was hanged in December. Though his unrealistic plan went nowhere, it caused extreme panic among Southerners who feared John Brown was typical of Northern abolitionists.

Stephen Douglas was not successful at his run for the presidency in 1860.

As the Republicans grew in number, the Democratic Party was falling apart. Southern fire-eaters were at one end. Northern, pro-Union compromisers, such as Stephen Douglas, were at the other end. Davis now openly favored secession if slavery was interfered with. Davis and other Democrats who feared a Republican victory in 1860 had plenty of reason to worry. The Democratic convention in April 1860 failed to nominate a presidential candidate. The convention, held in Charleston, South Carolina, completely fell apart over the issue of popular sovereignty. Southern Democrats demanded legal protection over slavery. No single candidate could win the needed two-thirds majority of votes. Many Southern delegates walked out, and the convention ended without choosing a candidate.

The election of 1860 is the only election where both political parties had more than one candidate running for president. Each party had two candidates, which split the electoral and popular votes four ways instead of just two.

Democrats held another convention in June in Baltimore, Maryland. This time Stephen Douglas won the nomination. But pro-slavery extremists nominated their own candidate, anyway: The current U.S. vice president, John C. Breckinridge of Kentucky.

Jefferson Davis did not try to discourage the Democratic candidate split. He wanted several candidates running for president so that the Republican nominee would be unable to get a majority of electoral college votes in the main election. In that case, the vote would go to Congress. The Senate had a Democratic majority and could give the presidency to a pro-slavery Democrat.

Republicans nominated Abraham Lincoln, a humble but skillful speaker who was not as radical as his better-known opponent, William Seward. A fourth candidate also ran: John Bell represented the new National Constitutional Union Party, which was pro-Union and pro-Constitution. It took no stand on slavery.

Abraham Lincoln won the election with a huge percentage of the electoral vote, even though Stephen Douglas won a good share of the popular vote. Now the Southern states had to demonstrate if they were serious about secession or were only bluffing. It didn't take long to find out: South Carolina, home to the most radical fire-eaters, seceded on December 20, 1860. Mississippi followed on January 19, 1861.

Two days later, Jefferson Davis made his last appearance in the Senate. He then left Washington for home, giving up his U.S. citizenship and expecting to serve his new country, the Confederate States of America, as a military leader.

After South Carolina and Mississippi, the next five states to secede were Georgia, Alabama, Florida, Texas, and Louisiana. When delegates from these states met in Montgomery, Alabama, to form a new government, Jefferson Davis was the only man they seriously considered for president of

Inauguration of Jefferson Davis on February 18, 1861.

the Confederate States of America. Jefferson told Varina the news as if it were a death sentence. However, he accepted the position all the same.

*The attack on
Fort Sumter
began the
Civil War.*

Davis still hoped secession could be accomplished peacefully, without war. The population of the slave-holding states was less than half that of the free states, and he knew that many Southerners did not want to leave the Union.

As Confederate president, Davis offered to buy all federal property in the Confederate states from the United States, such as Fort Sumter in the harbor of Charleston, South Carolina. But President

Lincoln refused to recognize the Confederacy as a new country.

U.S. soldiers were stationed at Fort Sumter, and on April 10, 1861, the Confederate government demanded they surrender. The Union soldiers refused, and on April 12, the Confederates began firing on the fort. Fort Sumter surrendered the next day.

President Lincoln called for volunteers to put down what he considered to be a rebellion. No one imagined that by the time the conflict was over, well over half a million Americans, mostly young men, would be dead. ✤

8 ANOTHER FLAG UNFURLED!

⁓❧⁓

At last, we are
A nation among nations; and the world
Shall soon behold in many a distant port
Another flag unfurled! ...
(from a poem by Confederate poet Henry Timrod)

As President Lincoln called on military volunteers, Virginia, North Carolina, Tennessee, and Arkansas joined the Confederacy. Virginia was especially important to Davis. He sent Confederate Vice President Alexander Stephens to Virginia to convince the state to join the South. Virginia was the home of patriot heroes (and slave owners) George Washington and Thomas Jefferson. Davis considered himself and other secessionists to be dutifully following their example in the fight against tyranny.

Young men dressed as Confederate soldiers in a
re-enactment of the Battle of Chancellorsville.

Virginians offered their capital, Richmond, to serve as the Confederate capital, placing the Confederate and Union capital cities just 100 miles (160 kilometers) apart. Richmond was a major slave market with a population of 40,000. Railroad lines crisscrossed the city, and a large iron works company was located there. This type of industry was rare in the South, but would be needed to manufacture weapons for the war.

Tredegar Iron Works in Richmond, Virginia, was the main source of cannons, railroad rails, and other weapons for the South. By 1863, Tredegar employed nearly 2,500 people. The company also operated shoe-making shops, a sawmill, a firebrick factory, and canal boats.

The main product the South had was cotton. They couldn't fight a war with it, but Davis and his government hoped cotton was important enough to England's industrial mills that the British would come to the Confederates' aid. The federal government, however, blocked Southern ports to keep ships from coming and going, including those with cotton to sell. Ships sometimes snuck through it, but the blockade seriously damaged the South's economy.

Davis arrived in Richmond near the end of May 1861, followed by his family in June. They moved into a large, gray stucco home that, despite its color, was called the White House. Varina received

The Confederate "White House" in Richmond, Virginia

guests nightly and enjoyed her hostess duties as Confederate First Lady. In December of that year, she gave birth to their fifth child, William Howell Davis.

After the surrender of Fort Sumter, Davis tried to prepare Southern troops for war, even though there weren't enough weapons for all the soldiers. General Joseph E. Johnston led the Virginia troops along with Generals Pierre Gustave Toutant de Beauregard and Robert E. Lee, Davis's friend from West Point. Another friend from West Point, General

Most battles of the Civil War were fought in the South.

Albert Sidney Johnston, was put in charge of defending states to the west of the fort.

In July, the Northern and Southern armies

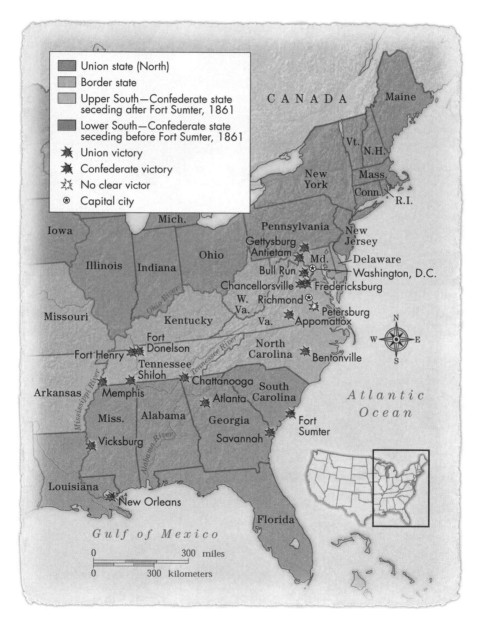

Map legend:
- Union state (North)
- Border state
- Upper South—Confederate state seceding after Fort Sumter, 1861
- Lower South—Confederate state seceding before Fort Sumter, 1861
- ✴ Union victory
- ✴ Confederate victory
- ✴ No clear victor
- ⊛ Capital city

CANADA

Maine

Vt. N.H.

New York

Mass.

Conn.

R.I.

Iowa

Mich.

Pennsylvania

New Jersey

Illinois

Indiana

Ohio

Gettysburg

Antietam

Md.

Delaware

Bull Run

Washington, D.C.

Chancellorsville

Fredericksburg

W. Va.

Richmond

Missouri

Kentucky

Va.

Petersburg

Appomattox

Fort Donelson

North Carolina

Bentonville

Fort Henry

Tennessee

Shiloh

Chattanooga

Arkansas

Memphis

Atlanta

South Carolina

Atlantic Ocean

Miss.

Alabama

Georgia

Fort Sumter

Vicksburg

Savannah

Louisiana

New Orleans

Florida

Ohio River

Tennessee River

Mississippi River

Alabama River

N W E S

Gulf of Mexico

0   300 miles

0   300 kilometers

finally faced each other at the First Battle of Bull Run near Manassas, Virginia. Under Generals Beauregard, Johnston, and Thomas "Stonewall" Jackson, the Confederates pushed Union troops into retreat. Both Davis and Lincoln, recognizing the tough fight that lay ahead, called for a draft, which required men to join the army. But the South didn't actually enact a draft until the next year. The North didn't have a draft until the year after that.

The Confederate government was organized much like that of the United States, though its Constitution made sure to clearly approve slavery. Davis did have a secretary of war, yet he spent much of the next four years directing the South's war efforts himself. Davis also managed to function daily as president, although he continued to suffer frequent attacks of malarial illness.

Davis could be quick tempered. He admitted his temper could get the best of him and cause him to hurl verbal attacks against people. He also found it difficult to share the work of running the war and the government with his Cabinet.

Vice President Stephens came to greatly resent Davis, and he spent the last part of the war encouraging anti-Davis governors, such as Georgia's Joseph Brown, to resist the draft laws. But Davis, who served purely out of duty to the Confederate cause, seldom allowed criticism to influence his

On New Year's Day 1862, Jefferson and Varina Davis held an open house in Richmond for any citizens who wanted to come. The open house had been a traditional New Year's event at the White House in Washington, D.C., since the presidency of Thomas Jefferson. This tradition continued until the early 1930s.

decisions. As 1861 ended, he was relieved that there had been no successful invasions of the South. He had full confidence in his commanders.

As the new year began, the Union was building up its army under General George McClellan, with an eye on Richmond. In the West, Union General Ulysses S. Grant inflicted on the Confederates what would be the first of many defeats for the South.

Grant captured Fort Donelson in Tennessee in February, then met General Albert Sidney Johnston's troops at Shiloh in April. The bloody two-day Battle of Shiloh left General Johnston and thousands of men from each army dead. Davis wept at the loss of both a friend and a general he depended upon.

By this time, Union troops were closing in on Richmond, but they were pushed back during the course of several battles in May and June. Though the capital remained safe, General Joe Johnston was wounded in June. Davis then appointed Robert E. Lee head of the Virginia army. In August, Lee won the Second Battle of Bull Run and decided to go on the offensive into Maryland.

On September 17, 1862, Lee's Army of Northern Virginia met the Union forces of General George McClellan along Antietam Creek, near Sharpsburg, Maryland. Here 23,000 men were killed or wounded in the bloodiest day of the war. In fact, it remains the bloodiest day in U.S. history.

In spite of the loss at Antietam, Jefferson Davis was happy with Lee because he was willing to go on the offensive. Davis came to rely heavily on Lee's opinions—the general was capable, modest, and loyal. And like Davis, Robert E. Lee put the Confederate cause ahead of his own military career.

Robert E. Lee (second from left) led his troops in many military battles.

Davis also had great confidence in General Thomas "Stonewall" Jackson. Jackson aided in Lee's substantial victory at Fredericksburg in December 1862. This victory increased the confidence of Lee's Army of Northern Virginia and led to the invasion of the North the following summer. But the West was another story.

Confederate control of the Mississippi River was essential in order for troops and supplies to pass to the West. The Southern army often had trouble supplying enough troops to defend areas under attack, and cooperation between generals was poor. Despite losses in 1862, most areas of the Confederacy remained safe, and Jefferson Davis still believed that the new nation would prevail.

On January 1, 1863, Lincoln's Emancipation Proclamation took effect, declaring slaves in the 11 rebellious Southern states to be free. Jefferson Davis was furious. Rather than see slavery as an institution that had split the country in two, Davis said it was Lincoln's policies toward the South that were destroying the Union.

Jefferson Davis put in long days as the Confederate president, despite his poor health. Just as he found a loyal adviser on army matters in General Lee, Davis also grew to count on the advice and friendship of Judah Benjamin, his secretary of state. Benjamin's keen intelligence

Jefferson Jr. (left to right), Margaret, William, and Varina Anne were an important part of Davis's life.

and cheerful personality lifted Davis's often heavy spirits. Davis also found relief from his worries by horseback riding, sometimes for hours at a time. At home, his children helped him forget his troubles—one visitor remarked that the Davis children's favorite playmate was their father.

In May 1863, General Lee enjoyed a bittersweet victory at Chancellorsville in Virginia. The military win was countered by the death of reliable Stonewall Jackson. Lee was devasted by the loss of Jackson, but didn't have time to mourn. Lee wanted to carry the momentum north and let his troops "feed" off the Union for a change. By this time, much of the South, including the soldiers, was suffering from lack of food and other necessities. Davis and Lee wanted Northern citizens to experience the same suffering.

The rate of Confederate soldiers who deserted, or left their units, had become a serious problem. Many were worried about family members who needed help with growing or harvesting crops. Desertion plagued the Union troops as well, but the North had many more men to replace those who left.

By July 1863, Robert E. Lee's troops had reached southern Pennsylvania. They were stopped at the town of Gettysburg by the Union army of Major General George G. Meade. The three-day battle that followed left more than 50,000 men dead and wounded, and it was made famous by Abraham Lincoln in his "Gettysburg Address," which honored the battle's fallen soldiers.

In the West, Ulysses S. Grant spent weeks trying to capture Vicksburg, Mississippi. The city finally surrendered on July 4. By September, most of Tennessee was in Union hands, and Union troops were 50 miles (80 kilometers) from Richmond, Virginia.

In October, Davis traveled to Alabama to fix the problems between his officers and encourage the soldiers and citizens of the West. He visited his family members in Mississippi and saw the ruins of the city of Jackson, burned by invading Union troops. As he traveled, Davis always took time to speak with

soldiers, citizens, and slaves. He came away from his trip with a high level of support, despite some criticism from other Confederate leaders.

Soldiers fought for three days at the Battle of Gettysburg in 1863.

At the end of 1863, Union troops occupied Kentucky, Missouri, much of Tennessee and Arkansas, southern Louisiana, and Virginia, and the coasts of the Carolinas. Davis still expressed confidence in the shrinking Confederacy, but the situation would only worsen in 1864. ஓ

9 FLIGHT THROUGH THE FALLING SOUTH

❦

By 1864, Union troops outnumbered Southern soldiers two to one. President Lincoln now put Ulysses S. Grant in charge of the entire Union Army. Grant had no fear of facing the enemy and planned a complex five-pronged offensive. Rather than try to capture a particular city, the Union generals would pursue the Confederate armies themselves, in an attempt to wear down the soldiers and exhaust their limited resources.

The Overland Campaign, in which Grant's Army of the Potomac drove Robert E. Lee's Army of Northern Virginia through central Virginia for six weeks, began in early May. Lee tried to break Grant's charge as Grant unsuccessfully tried to wear down the Southerners during 42 days of vicious, non-stop

Soldiers fought in battle after battle despite being exhausted and hungry.

fighting. More than 80,000 soldiers lost their lives.

Confederate General Joe Johnston, instructed to face Union Commander William Tecumseh Sherman, worried Davis with constant retreats toward Atlanta. That city would be quite a trophy for Sherman; it was a transportation hub with several railroad lines. If taken, it would open up much of Georgia and South Carolina for the Union. In mid-summer, Davis relieved Johnston of his command and replaced him with General John B. Hood. In doing so, Davis created a bitter enemy in Joe Johnston. Hood was now given the job of stopping Sherman.

General John B. Hood was aggresive and fought hard. In 1863, he was wounded in the Battle of Gettysburg. Two months later, at the Battle of Chickamauga, Hood was wounded again. Though he was first pronounced dead, surgeons were able to save him by amputating his right leg.

Meanwhile, tragedy struck the Davis family once again. In April, their 5-year-old son Joe was playing at the Richmond White House when he fell from a 12-foot-high (3.6-meter-high) railing. Joe died later that day from a head injury. His parents were grief-stricken. Varina's close friend Mary Chesnut wrote in her diary that Jefferson Davis spent the entire night pacing the floor of his house. Less than two months later, Varina gave birth to their sixth child and second daughter, Varina Anne. Their joy was mixed with grief over Joe's death as well as worry about Richmond coming under direct attack.

Even though Davis was extrememly thin that summer, he remained vigorous. Davis happily greeted 1,000 Confederate soldiers and recently released prisoners of war returning to Richmond, but he had to tell them that they would be needed back at the front lines. In fact, Davis had to admit, boys as young as 13 or 14 were also needed. Confederate supplies were not reliable, and some soldiers, though tough, were existing on few rations.

Varina Anne Davis was known as the "Daughter of the Confederacy."

Fighting raged around Richmond, but the city remained untouched. General Hood had put up a fight in Georgia, but too much ground had been lost by the time he was given command. Atlanta took a beating and fell to Sherman in early September. From there, Sherman decided to march his entire army southeast toward Savannah. General Ulysses S. Grant instructed Sherman to damage as many war supplies as possible in order to encourage surrender and an

Southern cities were left in shambles after battles were finished and soldiers moved on.

end to the war. Sherman's army cut a 60-mile-wide (96-wide-kilometer) path of destruction across the Georgia countryside.

Davis went south to Georgia, hoping to stir up enthusiasm among both civilians and soldiers to resist the Union invasion. As he reviewed battle-weary troops in Macon, Georgia, there were no cheers for the president, only the required salutes.

For the next several months, Davis would plead with Southerners to rally to the Confederate cause and resist, though they were often without food or shoes. Desertion continued to shrink the Confederate troops. Davis still thought that if the deserters would return to their ranks, the war could be turned around. He was completely dedicated to the Confederate cause and refused to see that his own people were tired, hungry, grieving for lost loved ones, and sick of war.

The governor of North Carolina, Zebulon Vance, supported the war, but didn't like how Davis was running things. North Carolina, with a large population of peaceful Quakers, was the last Southern state to secede. As desertion shrank the number of Confederate troops, Vance remarked, "It shows what I have always believed, that the great popular heart is not now and never has been in this war. It was a revolution of the politicians, not the people."

Despite pockets of Southern support in the North, antiwar and anti-Lincoln sentiment would not be enough to end the war peacefully. The fall of Atlanta rallied most Northerners to the cause of defeating the rebellious South and contributed significantly to the reelection of Abraham Lincoln in 1864.

Amid the frights and struggles of the dying

> *Prices for everyday items were outrageous and getting worse. Flour went up to $1,500 a barrel, a hen cost $50, and a pound of butter $20. Those prices were in Confederate paper dollars, which had become worthless. The Davis family sold their carriages and as many horses as they could spare, as well as silver, furniture, and paintings to earn some extra money.*

Confederacy, Varina Davis was determined to have a joyous Christmas with her family. She took much pleasure in their new baby, Varina Anne—nickamed "Winnie"—and managed to set aside small items for the children's and servants' Christmas gifts. She organized a Christmas party for children at a Richmond orphanage, and the Davis family took them a Christmas tree, along with donated gifts of used and repaired toys. But, after the merry holiday, it was back to the reality of war.

By 1865, President Davis had lost the support of his government officials, both state and national. Many believed that he should turn over control of the war to Robert E. Lee, who was respected throughout the South. Davis had made enough mistakes in judgment in the past concerning his generals that he agreed to make Lee "general in chief" of all Southern armies.

In January, with Davis's approval, Vice President Stephens approached President Lincoln about terms for peace. The men met aboard the Union gunboat *River Queen* at Hampton Roads, Virginia. But

Lincoln was firm on his terms: There must be an immediate cease-fire, the Confederacy must be dissolved, and all slaves must be freed. "The war will cease on the part of the Government, whenever it shall have ceased on the part of those who began it," Lincoln said.

In a public speech on February 6, 1865, Davis defiantly declared that the South would never submit to the "disgrace of surrender." In fact, he predicted that Southern armies would yet "compel the Yankees, in less than twelve months, to petition us for peace on our own terms."

Confederate money became worthless by the end of the war.

Davis then sent representatives to France and England to ask for last-minute help. He even asked whether recognition and support would come if the Confederate states were to abolish slavery on their own—in complete disregard of why they fought. But neither country wanted to get involved in what appeared to be a lost cause.

By early 1865, the armies of Lee and Grant still had not resolved their drawn-out battle. Both armies were clustered around Petersburg, Virginia, south of Richmond. Sherman had cut a swath of destruction through Georgia and South Carolina and was on his way to join Grant in Virginia.

Early in April, Robert E. Lee's weak forces abandoned Richmond and Petersburg and began a retreat to the southwest. Union forces then entered and secured Richmond while Grant searched for Lee, who was hoping to meet up with Johnston. But Union General Phillip H. Sheridan's men reached the railroad first and blocked Lee's only line of advance. On April 9, Generals Ulysses S. Grant and Robert E. Lee met at the home of the McLean family in the village of Appomattox Courthouse, Virginia. There, Lee surrendered, accepting Grant's terms.

Jefferson Davis, however, was unaware of Lee's surrender. As Lee and Grant discussed the end of the war, Davis had already fled Richmond and

Confederate General Lee signing the surrender at Appomattox in 1865.

was making his way south with plans to set up the Confederate government elsewhere. Davis had urged his commanders to fight on, using any tactics necessary. Once his army surrendered, Robert E. Lee told his men to return home peacefully. ✑

10 I Have Not Repented!

❧⚬✦⚬❧

The Richmond that welcomed Jefferson Davis as Confederate president in 1861 was very different from the one he fled nearly four years later. The city's hungry citizens had recently looted warehouses and shops, looking for food; some were reduced to eating rats to survive. Among his people, Davis went from being a symbol of Southern pride and independence to one of defeat and misery.

Davis was in church the Sunday morning of April 2, 1865, when he received a message from General Lee telling him to leave the city. Varina and the children had left a few days earlier for Charlotte, North Carolina. Jefferson gave his wife all but $5 of his remaining gold money and showed her how to use a gun before they said a tearful goodbye.

Citizens grabbed whatever belongings they could and watched the city of Richmond burn in 1865.

Jefferson Davis, though not yet 60, looked like an old man. His cheekbones stuck out from his thin, lined face, and his eye that pained him so much was now cloudy and blind. Leaving family belongings behind, Davis met his Cabinet at the railroad station that evening to begin their journey south. Included in the presidential caravan was the Confederate treasury, estimated at half a million dollars in gold and silver.

The Confederate leaders wondered what their fate would be if captured: Would they be arrested? Hanged as traitors? When asked how he planned to handle the fleeing Confederate leaders, Abraham Lincoln said, "That door will be left open; let them go!"

Davis (sitting) and his Cabinet began their long journey south.

Davis and his group weren't always well received as they traveled south. Some people feared that Union troops would punish anyone who sheltered the Confederate leaders. In mid-April in Greensboro, North Carolina, Davis was still figuring ways to continue the war. By now Generals Johnston and Beauregard had arrived. Johnston bluntly told Davis that "it would be the greatest of human crimes" to continue fighting.

On April 13, Davis learned of Lee's surrender at Appomattox and wept. When, several days later, he learned that Lincoln had been assassinated, Davis knew the Confederacy was over. Mercy would be hard to come by from Lincoln's successor, Andrew Johnson. Johnson, who had been against secession, placed a $100,000 reward on Davis's head. Jefferson Davis was now a wanted man.

By May 7, Davis had met up with the caravan of "Mrs. Jones"—the name his wife was traveling under. The family rode together for three days, though they were slowed down as Union troops closed in on them. Much of Davis's staff had gone their separate ways, each taking some of the treasury to deposit in banks for later use by a possible new Confederate government.

Just before dawn on May 10, 1865, shots rang out in the Davis family camp. Davis was wearing a large poncho over which Varina had thrown her shawl as

Jefferson Davis was watched by two guards at all times.

he stepped out of their tent. Rumors of Davis trying to disguise himself as a woman when he was captured hounded him for years.

Davis was sent to prison at Fort Monroe in Virginia, where security was extraordinarily tight. To prevent escape or feared rescue attempts, two guards paced his room night and day. Though thin and ill, Davis put up a fight when a blacksmith entered his cell to shackle his ankles. News of his treatment got out, and the fort's commander assigned a kindly doctor, John J. Craven, to attend to him. Dr. Craven requested removal of the shackles after five days. Craven and Davis became good friends, and the doctor marveled at the variety of topics Davis could easily discuss.

One year later, the federal government still had not brought charges against Jefferson Davis. Varina, who was living in Canada with the children, received permission from President Johnson to visit her husband in May 1866. Loud calls for Davis's release were heard from the North as well as the South after Dr. Craven wrote about his treatment in prison. Varina then went to President Johnson to plead for her husband. But when Johnson said Davis would likely be released if he requested a pardon, Varina knew her husband would choose prison.

Jefferson Davis didn't have to make that choice after all. Newspaper publisher Horace Greeley and other influential Northerners put up $100,000 to have Davis released on bail. After two years at Fort Monroe, Davis was free to await trial. Secretary of War Edwin Stanton and Davis's old friend William Seward, now secretary of state, wanted to see Davis tried for treason in a military court. But since the war was over, it was decided to try him in a civil court.

Davis was released from Fort Monroe exactly two years after his capture. Jefferson and Varina took a steamer to Richmond, where they were cheered and given the same room at the Spotswood

Jefferson Davis's thoughts and heart remained in the antebellum, or pre-Civil War South. However, Robert E. Lee wanted to put the war behind him. Lee even signed the Oath of Allegiance (a document declaring loyalty to the United States), which many Southerners— including Jefferson Davis—refused to sign.

Hotel that they stayed in when they arrived in 1861. On May 13, the couple left for Canada, where Jefferson would see his older children for the first time in two years.

Davis returned to Richmond in November 1867 for another court hearing. After a trip to Cuba to withdraw money that had been deposited for them, Davis and Varina traveled together through the South. The charges of treason against Davis were dropped on February 15, 1869, after President Andrew Johnson extended amnesty, or forgiveness, to all former Confederates.

Although Davis's courage and conduct at Fort Monroe had made him once again a hero to fellow Southerners, he was in desperate need of employment to support his family. Too proud to seek it for himself, Davis waited for offers to come to him. In 1869, a Memphis insurance company hired him to be its president. Varina and the children joined him in Memphis two years later. In 1872, tragedy struck again when their son William ("Billy") died of diphtheria just before his 11th birthday.

Davis lived and worked at Beauvoir.

The insurance company went out of business in 1874. Davis was greatly relieved when a New York publisher asked him to write his war memoirs. A family friend and widow, Sarah Dorsey, offered Davis use of a small house on her Mississippi Gulf Coast plantation, called Beauvoir, in which to live and write.

Jefferson Davis spent four years writing his memoirs, *The Rise and Fall of the Confederate Government.* It was available in 1881 and sold well on into the 20th century. Much of his book discussed his favorite subject from long ago: how secession and the Confederacy were similar to the great American Revolution.

After Mrs. Dorsey died, Davis discovered she'd willed her estate to him. He lived quietly at Beauvoir until he was invited to address the Mississippi legislature in 1884. "I have not repented," he told the state legislators, and claimed he would do it all over again, if necessary. Other cities invited him, as well. In Savannah, he encouraged his cheering listeners to remain proud of the Confederacy.

Jefferson Davis died December 6, 1889, and was buried in New Orleans, Louisiana. Newspapers spoke of his dedication to the Southern cause. *The New York Times*, which had called for his execution after the war, said, "The South loves his memory, as it should love it."

In 1890, Varina Davis wrote a book about her husband's life. In May 1893, she returned to Richmond for the reburial of Jefferson Davis's body in Richmond's Hollywood Cemetery. No doubt Davis would have approved. Virginia was where Confederate greats such as Robert E. Lee and Stonewall Jackson were buried, as well as heroes

such as George Washington and Thomas Jefferson—two of America's greatest patriots. After all, an American patriot is what Jefferson Davis always claimed to be. ᔈ

DAVIS'S LIFE

1808

Jefferson F. Davis born in Christian County, Kentucky, June 3

1828

Graduates from the U.S. Military Academy at West Point; reports for duty at Jefferson Barracks near St. Louis, Missouri

1834

Promoted to first lieutenant and assigned to special Army unit, the First Dragoons in present-day Oklahoma

1805

1830

1821

Central American countries gain independence from Spain

1809

Louis Braille of France, inventor of a writing system for the blind, is born

1833

Great Britain abolishes slavery

WORLD EVENTS

1835

Marries Sarah Knox Taylor, who dies three months later of malaria

1845

Marries Varina Banks Howell; elected to U.S. House of Representatives

1846

Commissioned as a colonel to lead Mississippi volunteers in Mexican War; participates in successful battle at Monterrey, Mexico, in September

1840

1836

Texans defeat Mexican troops at San Jacinto after a deadly battle at the Alamo

1846

Irish potato famine reaches its worst

DAVIS'S LIFE

1851

Resigns from Senate
to run for governor of
Mississippi; loses
election

1847

Participates in successful
battle (though wounded)
at Buena Vista, Mexico,
in February; appointed
to fill vacancy as U.S.
senator for Mississippi

1850

1848

*The Communist
Manifesto* by
German writer
Karl Marx is wide-
ly distributed

1850

Jeans are invented
by Levi Strauss, a
German who moved
to California during
the gold rush

WORLD EVENTS

1853

Appointed secretary of war by President Franklin Pierce

1857

Reelected to Senate

1861

Resigns from Senate to serve as president of the Confederate States of America

1860

1856

The Treaty of Paris ends the Crimean War

1858

English scientist Charles Darwin presents his theory of evolution

1860

Austrian composer Gustav Mahler is born in Kalischt (now in Austria)

DAVIS'S LIFE

1867

Released from prison

1865

General Robert E. Lee surrenders; Davis and his Confederate Cabinet flee Richmond; Davis is captured in May and imprisoned at Fort Monroe in Virginia for two years

1861

Moves to Richmond, Virginia, the capital of the Confederacy; serves as president of the Confederacy for four years

1865

1870

1865

Lewis Carroll writes *Alice's Adventures in Wonderland*

1869

The periodic table of elements is invented

WORLD EVENTS

1881

Publishes his book on
the Confederacy

1889

Dies at Beauvoir, on
the Mississippi Gulf
Coast; buried in New
Orleans, Louisiana

1893

Body is reburied in
Richmond, Virginia

1890

1879

Electric lights are
invented

1893

Women gain voting
privileges in New
Zealand, the first
country to take such
a step

NICKNAME: "Jeff" Davis

DATE OF BIRTH: June 3, 1808

BIRTHPLACE: Christian County, Kentucky

FATHER: Samuel Emory Davis
(1756-1824)

MOTHER: Jane Cook Davis (?1760-1845)

EDUCATION: St. Thomas College;
Wilkinson County Academy;
Transylvania University;
U.S. Military Academy

SPOUSES: Sarah Knox Taylor (1814-1835);
married June 1835
Varina Banks Howell (1826-
1906); married February 1845

CHILDREN: Samuel Emory (1852-1854)
Margaret "Maggie" Howell
(1855-1909)
Jefferson Junior (1857-1878)
Joseph Evan (1859-1864)
William Howell (1861-1872)
Varina "Winnie" Anne
(1864-1898)

DATE OF DEATH: December 6, 1889

PLACE OF BURIAL: Richmond, Virginia

IN THE LIBRARY

Carter, E.J. *Jefferson Davis.* Chicago: Heinemann Library, 2004.

Frazier, Joey. *Jefferson Davis: Confederate President.* Philadelphia: Chelsea House Publishers, 2000.

Ingram, W. Scott. *Jefferson Davis.* Woodbridge, Conn.: Blackbirch Press, 2002.

Gaines, Ann. *The Confederacy and the Civil War in American History.* Berkeley Heights, N.J.: Enslow Publishers, 2000.

Golay, Michael. *Civil War.* New York: Facts on File, 2003.

Murray, Aaron R. *Civil War: Battles and Leaders.* New York: DK Publications, 2004.

Wisler, G. Clifton. *When Johnny Went Marching: Young Americans Fight the Civil War.* New York: HarperCollins Publications, 2001.

ON THE WEB

For more information on *Jefferson Davis*, use FactHound to track down Web sites related to this book.

1. Go to *www.facthound.com*
2. Type in a search word related to this book or this book ID: 0756508177
3. Click on the *Fetch It* button.

FactHound will find the best Web sites for you.

HISTORIC SITES

Jefferson Davis Memorial State Historic Site
338 Jeff Davis Park Road
Fitzgerald, GA 31750
912/831-2335
To view the Jefferson Davis Memorial, visit a Civil War Museum, and hike nature trails

The National Civil War Museum
One Lincoln Circle at Reservoir Park
P.O. Box 1861
Harrisburg, PA 17105
717/260-1861
To learn more about the Civil War

abolitionist
someone who supported the banning of slavery

annexation
the addition of another territory to an existing country
or state

arsenal
a place where guns and ammunition are made or stored

blockade
the use of warships to shut down trade or
communication with a port or ports

compromise
an agreement that is reached by both sides giving up
part of what they want

Confederacy
the Southern states that fought against the Northern
states in the Civil War; also called the Confederate
States of America

constituents
people who are represented by someone else

Constitution
the document stating the basic laws of the United States

diphtheria
a serious disease caused by bacteria

electoral college
a group of people who elect the U.S. president; each
state is given a certain number of electoral votes; the
candidate who receives the most votes from the people
in a state is awarded that state's electoral votes.

exports
things made or grown in one country and sold in
another country

imports
to bring in goods from another country

inauguration
a ceremony at which a president is sworn into office

latitude
an east-west line around Earth to measure distance from the equator

legislature
the part of government that makes or changes laws

Manifest Destiny
the belief that Americans had the right to the western land all the way to the Pacific Ocean

memoirs
written documentation of a life story

minié ball
a bullet with a cone-shaped head used in muzzle-loading rifles

nomination
the process of choosing a candidate for office

pardon
act that forgives a crime, so that the person who committed the crime is not punished

secede
withdrawal from a group

tactics
plans or methods to win a game or battle (or achieve a goal)

tariff
a tax placed on certain foreign goods entering a country

treason
an attempt to betray one's own country

zealous
showing extreme interest or enthusiasm for a subject

Chapter 1

Page 9, line 6: Davis, Jefferson. "Farewell Address to the U.S. Senate." *The Papers of Jefferson Davis, Volume 7: 1861.* Baton Rouge, LA: Louisiana State University Press, 1992, pp. 18–23.

Page 10, line 21: Ibid.

Chapter 3

Page 20, line 23: Cooper, William J. *Jefferson Davis, American.* New York: Alfred A. Knopf, 2000, p. 55.

Chapter 4

Page 30, line 8: Davis, Jefferson. "Varina Banks Howell Davis." *The Papers of Jefferson Davis , Volume 2: June 1841–July 1846.* Baton Rouge, LA: Louisiana State University Press, 1987, pp. 52–53.

Chapter 7

Page 51, line 8: Catton, William, and Bruce Catton. *Two Roads to Sumter.* New York: McGraw Hill Book Co. Inc., 1963, p. 130.

Page 53, line 17: Ibid., p. 166.

Page 54, line 6: Ibid., p. 168.

Page 55, line 16: Davis, Jefferson. "Speech at Boston, Mass." *The Papers of Jefferson Davis, Volume 6: 1856–1860.* Baton Rouge, LA: Louisiana State University Press, 1989, p. 587.

Chapter 8

Page 65, line 1: Timrod, Henry. "Ethnogenesis" (verse 1: lines 4-7). "The Poems of Henry Timrod." *Documenting the American South.* http://docsouth.unc.edu/timrod/timrod.html.

Chapter 9

Page 81, line 17: Davis, Burke. *The Long Surrender.* New York: Random House, 1985, p. 83.

Page 83, line 3: Harris, William C. "The Hampton Road Peace Conference: A Final Test of Lincoln's Presidential Leadership." *Journal of the Abraham Lincoln Association (JALA)* 21.1 (Winter 2000). 23 Nov. 2004, http://jala.press.uiuc.edu/21.1/harris.html.

Page 83, line 9: McPherson, James M. *Battle Cry of Freedom: The Civil War Era.* New York: Oxford University Press, 1988, p. 824.

Chapter 10

Page 88, line 14: Davis, Burke. *The Long Surrender.* New York: Random House, 1985, p. 18.

Page 89, line 8: Ibid., p. 67.

Page 94, line 11: Ibid., p. 259.

Catton, William and Bruce. *Two Roads to Sumter.* New York: McGraw Hill Book Co. Inc., 1963.

The Civil War Homepage. http://www.civil-war.net

Cooper, William J. *Jefferson Davis, American.* New York: Alfred A. Knopf, 2000.

Davis, Burke. *The Long Surrender.* New York: Random House, 1985.

Jefferson Davis 1808-1889: President of the Confederate States of America. http://www.americancivilwar.com/south/jeffdavi.html

Morison, Samuel Eliot. *The Oxford History of the American People.* New York: Oxford University Press, 1965

The Papers of Jefferson Davis. http://jeffersondavis.rice.edu

Woodward, C. Vann. *Mary Chesnut's Civil War.* New Haven, Conn.: Yale University Press, 1981.

Jean Kinney Williams lives and writes in Cincinnati, Ohio. Her nonfiction books for children include several books in the Profiles of the Presidents series and the We the People series for Compass Point Books.